THE SUPREME COURT

THE SUPREME COURT

DILLON PRESS
New York

Maxwell Macmillan Canada
Toronto
Maxwell Macmillan International
New York   Oxford   Singapore   Sydney

By Catherine Reef

Photo Credits

John Reef: pages 2-3, 21, 25, 47, 54, 56, 57, and 64

UPI/Bettmann: pages 6, 12, 14, 23, 36, 40, 42, 59, and 60

Library of Congress Cataloging-in-Publication Data

Reef, Catherine.
    The Supreme Court / by Catherine Reef. — 1st ed.
      p. cm. — (Places in American history)
    Includes index.
    ISBN 0-87518-626-2   0-382-24722-1 (pbk.)
    1. United States. Supreme Court—History—Juvenile literature. 2.
Judicial power—United States—History—Juvenile literature. [1. United
States. Supreme Court. 2. Judicial power.] I. Title. II. Series.
KF8742.Z9R44 1994
347.73'26'09—dc20   93-21506
[347.3073509]

Summary: A history of the Supreme Court and the power of the judicial
branch of the United States government.

Dillon Press   Maxwell Macmillan Canada, Inc.
Macmillan Publishing Company   1200 Eglinton Avenue East
866 Third Avenue   Suite 200
New York, NY 10022   Don Mills, Ontario M3C 3N1

Macmillan Publishing Company is part of the Maxwell Communication Group
of Companies.

First edition

Printed in the United States of America

10 9 8 7 6 5 4 3 2 1

CONTENTS

CHAPTER 1

EQUAL JUSTICE
UNDER LAW

A cold wind blew through Washington, D.C., on January 25, 1993. The wind had pushed nearly every cloud from the sky, and the sun shone brightly on the clean, white marble of the Supreme Court building. Outside the nation's highest court, the American flag few at half-mast. Thurgood Marshall, a retired justice of the Supreme Court, had died of a heart attack at the age of 83. America was mourning this outstanding citizen.

Chief Justice William Rehnquist spoke about Marshall to the people assembled in the Court that morning—his fellow justices, lawyers, and members of the public. "Peacefully, and in the fullness of time, came the close of a life of unique

Justice Thurgood Marshall in 1991, shortly before his retirement

distinction," Rehnquist said.

The chief justice reviewed the highlights of Marshall's early life and career. "Born in Baltimore, Maryland, in 1908, Thurgood Marshall was the grandson of a Union soldier, his namesake, and a great-grandson of a slave," Rehnquist noted. Marshall earned high marks at Howard University Law School and went to work for the National Association for the Advancement of Colored People (NAACP), to promote racial equality. "In courthouses across the country, he became the champion of equal justice and equal opportunity for minorities," Rehnquist said. In 1953, Marshall made the nation listen when he argued for equality before the Supreme Court.

At that time, 17 states and the District of Columbia permitted segregated schools, schools that separated children by race. Segregation meant that young black people were often denied educational opportunities that white children took for granted. In one South Carolina school district, for example, the black children in two schools had no desks at all.

Because of segregation, children such as Linda Brown of Topeka, Kansas, could not attend schools in their own neighborhoods. Eight-year-old Linda attended an all-black school more than 20 city blocks from her home. Her walk to and from school was a dangerous one that took her through a railroad yard.

Linda's father, Oliver Brown, sued the Topeka Board of Education. He claimed that segregation violated Linda's rights as a citizen of the United States. In a Kansas courtroom, the Browns' lawyer argued that the Constitution, the "supreme law of the land," promises equal opportunities to all Americans. Segregated schools, said the lawyer, denied black children an equal chance for learning.

The Kansas court agreed that segregation could harm "the educational and mental development of Negro children." Still, Oliver Brown lost his case. The Constitution, the Kansas judges said, permitted segregated schools. The judges based their decision on an 1896 ruling stating that segregation was constitutional as long as facilities were "separate but equal." The Kansas judges found the schools in question to be equal in terms of teachers, lessons, and buildings. In Washington, D.C., South Carolina, and elsewhere, judges were reaching the same conclusion about school segregation. Many Americans believed these rulings to be wrong, and the NAACP went to work to get them reversed. It appeared that only by a Supreme Court ruling that segregation was unconstitutional could America's black children secure their right to an equal education.

The Supreme Court is a place where ordinary people make history. Bakers and business executives, scientists and drifters, parents like Oliver

Brown—men and women from many walks of life have asked the Supreme Court to review their legal cases. Supreme Court rulings can change the law of the land. The rulings have affected the lives of millions of people.

Most courts in the United States are trial courts, where a judge and jury hear testimony from witnesses. The Supreme Court is an appellate court. Its justices listen to lawyers explain the legal aspects of cases that have already been decided in the trial courts. The justices study the details of these cases to determine whether the trial courts—and the laws on which their verdicts were based—are in agreement with the Constitution. The justices discuss each case privately and then vote to reach a decision.

In December 1953, the Supreme Court heard arguments in the case known as *Brown v. Board of Education*. (The *v.* in the name of a legal case stands for "versus," which means "against.") Thurgood Marshall spoke for the black children.

Justice Marshall in front of the Supreme Court during the school segregation crisis

Marshall told about the many communities he had visited where black and white children mingled freely outside of school. "They play in the streets together, they play on their farms together, they go down the road together," he said. It was the racism of adults, Marshall explained, that kept the children apart in school.

In his deep voice, Marshall concluded that if the Supreme Court voted to keep segregation, it would be telling America "that for some reason Negroes are inferior to all other human beings."

The Supreme Court justices, nine of the nation's foremost legal experts, took five months to announce the outcome of their vote. The nation waited. At last, on May 17, 1954, Chief Justice Earl Warren read their unanimous opinion. "School segregation by state law causes a feeling of inferiority in black children," Warren stated. It is a feeling "that inflicts damage to their hearts and minds that may never be undone." The Court ruled that such laws violate the Constitution.

Warren's words marked a turning point in American history. They opened the doors of the nation's public schools to children of all races.

The decision in the case of *Brown v. Board of*

As a result of the 1954 Supreme Court decision, children in Washington, D.C., were integrated into classrooms.

Education made history, but for the Supreme Court it was business as usual. Week after week, Supreme Court decisions set guidelines that the federal, state, and local governments must follow. Year after year, the Court works to secure justice for all Americans.

Supreme Court decisions have protected people's civil rights, freedom of speech, and right to privacy. They have regulated business practices and clarified the role of religion in public life. As the head of the judicial branch of the federal government, the Supreme Court has defined the powers of Congress and the president.

The 1954 decision was one in a long string of victories for Thurgood Marshall. As an attorney, he won 29 civil rights cases in the Supreme Court. This achievement prompted President Lyndon B. Johnson, in 1967, to name Marshall the first African-American Supreme Court justice. Upon joining the Court, Marshall expressed his deep faith in his nation. "I shall ever be mindful of my obligation to the Constitution," he said, "and to the goal of equal justice under law."

Thurgood Marshall retired from the Supreme Court in 1991. "I'm old," he told a group of reporters. "I'm getting old and coming apart."

Like Marshall, all of the Supreme Court justices have a great deal of legal knowledge and experience. Before joining the Court, most worked as judges, law professors, or government officials. One justice, William Howard Taft, served as president of the United States. Appointed by the president and approved by the Senate, Supreme Court justices may hold their positions for life.

At the Supreme Court, people see the government at work. The justices, attired in black robes, sit behind a curved mahogany bench. Some rock back in their tall chairs to think and listen and concentrate, while others lean forward. Attorneys who are arguing cases before the Court stand at a wooden podium facing the justices' bench. They have 30 minutes to convince the justices that their viewpoint is correct. The justices frequently interrupt with questions that make for a lively give-and-take session.

In Court, the justices also announce their opinions on cases they heard weeks or months earlier. Visitors never know ahead of time if they will hear the justices read a decision that creates controversy or makes history.

On January 25, 1993, the justices heard no cases. Instead, they joined with their fellow Americans to remember their friend and colleague Thurgood Marshall. "The members of this Court will miss Justice Marshall's wit, warmth, and humor," said Chief Justice Rehnquist. "I speak for them in expressing our sympathy to Mrs. Marshall, her sons, Thurgood and John, the remainder of the Marshall family, and all those whose lives were touched by this extraordinary man."

CHAPTER 2

THE STORM CENTER

Throughout the summer of 1787, Philadelphia was noisy with debate. Delegates from 12 of the 13 states had gathered in this Pennsylvania city. They had taken on an enormous job: drafting the Constitution. They had come together to organize the government of the United States.

George Washington had called the United States a country with "thirteen heads." Now, the delegates were proving him correct. Every delegate had his own ideas about how the government should operate. As he presided over this long meeting, known as the Constitutional Convention, Washington heard his countrymen argue over how many representatives in Congress each state should have. They haggled over the best way to choose a national leader. But when the talk turned to the need for federal courts, everyone agreed. America needed such courts to settle disputes between the people of different states or cases involving the U.S. government.

The writers of the Constitution called for a judicial branch of government consisting of one Supreme Court and "such inferior courts as the Congress may from time to time ordain and establish." They left it up to Congress to decide the number of lower courts in the system. To keep the Supreme Court from becoming too powerful, the founding fathers assigned the president the task of appointing its justices. It became the Senate's job to confirm or reject the justices that the president appointed.

By September 1788, the states had ratified, or accepted, the Constitution. Soon, the new Congress was hard at work on the First Judiciary Act, a law outlining the structure of the federal court system. The new law called for 13 district courts, one in each state, to make up the lowest level of the system. At the next level would be three judicial circuits: East, Middle, and West, each with its own court.

Congress decided that the Supreme Court would have one chief justice and five associate justices. The justices would meet in the nation's capital twice a year. One term was to begin on the first Monday in February, the other on the first Monday in August. The First Judiciary Act outlined some of the justices' duties and powers as well. For example, the justices had to "ride circuit." The law required them to hear cases in the district and circuit courts, spending long periods on the road. The law gave the Court the power to issue writs of mandamus—direct, written orders to public officials.

George Washington, now president of the United States, signed the First Judiciary Act into law in 1789, and promptly sent Congress the

A bust of John Jay, the first chief justice of the United States, in the lobby of the Supreme Court

names of his first Supreme Court appointments. Two days later, the Senate confirmed Washington's choices. Washington had named John Jay, a noted statesman and attorney from New York, to be the first chief justice. Washington expressed his "singular pleasure" that such a well-respected person would head the Court. Washington's praise, replied Jay, "will never cease to excite my best endeavor."

The Supreme Court first met on February 1, 1790, in New York City, then the nation's capital. But with no cases to decide, the justices ended their session nine days later. Their August meeting lasted only two days. And after the capital was moved to Philadelphia in 1791, outbreaks of yellow fever kept the Court from holding three of its summer sessions.

The Supreme Court faced further setbacks during its first years. Two justices resigned rather than continue riding circuit. Thousands of miles of stagecoach travel, bad roads, poor food, and unclean lodgings had taken a toll on their health. John Jay, too, lost his excitement. He resigned from the Supreme Court in 1795 to serve as governor of New York.

By 1801, the government had moved to its new capital, Washington, D.C. The Supreme Court was meeting in the basement of the unfinished U.S. Capitol, and John Marshall was the chief justice. A man of unusual wisdom, Marshall

*When Washington, D.C., became the nation's capital, the Supreme
Court would meet in the basement of the unfinished Capitol building.*

is remembered as "the great chief justice." The
Marshall Court decided a historic case known as
Marbury v. Madison, which established the
Supreme Court as the nation's authority on con-
stitutional matters.

The case had its beginnings in 1801, when a
new law called for additional federal judges in
the lower courts. President John Adams, soon to
leave office, hurried to appoint judges who
shared his political beliefs. Adams signed the
judges' appointments, and his secretary of state
delivered most of them—but not all. When the

next president, Thomas Jefferson, took office on March 4, several undelivered appointments were sitting on his desk. One was for a man named William Marbury.

It would have been a simple matter to deliver those documents. But Jefferson was not so sure he wanted to. He preferred to appoint judges of his own choosing. He asked his secretary of state, James Madison, to hold onto the undelivered appointments.

Marbury was determined to receive his commission, though, and he went to the Supreme Court. He asked the Court to issue a writ of mandamus, a document ordering the secretary of state to deliver his signed appointment. But instead of doing as Marbury asked, John Marshall and the other justices reviewed all of the legal aspects of the case.

On February 24, 1803, Marshall announced the Court's decision: Marbury had a right to receive his appointment. There was just one

John Marshall was chief justice for 35 years, during a time when the Supreme Court strengthened its role in American government. Marshall's statue is in the lobby of the Supreme Court.

problem. The Court could not make Madison deliver it. The First Judiciary Act, Marshall explained, was flawed. By giving the Supreme Court the power to issue writs of mandamus, Congress had gone beyond the guidelines set forth in the Constitution.

With that decision, the Supreme Court claimed the right to decide whether laws are constitutional, or in agreement with the Constitution, a right the Court exercises to this day. This is known as the right to judicial review. Chief Justice Marshall told his fellow Americans that it is the "duty of the judicial department to say what law is."

John Marshall served on the Supreme Court for 34 years, until his death in 1835. During his long career, Marshall saw the Court's size and responsibilities change. Congress reduced the number of justices to five in 1801, then raised it to seven in 1807. The number would reach nine in 1837. In its first years, the Court heard about 5 cases annually. By 1835, that number had grown to 35.

For years, the justices met in borrowed rooms. Yet throughout the history of the Supreme Court, they have been involved in the controversies of their day. As Oliver Wendell Holmes, a 20th-century justice, observed, "We are very quiet there, but it is the quiet of a storm center."

The storm that raged across the land in the 1850s was the issue of slavery. Many Americans in the South claimed they had a right to own African-American slaves. Others, largely in the North, insisted that slavery was wrong. People argued heatedly about the spread of slavery into new states and territories. With its decision in the Dred Scott case in 1854, the Supreme Court further divided Americans and damaged its own reputation.

Dred Scott was a slave from Missouri who sued his legal owner. As the slave of an army doctor, Scott had traveled with his owner to Illinois and Fort Snelling, Wisconsin Territory (now part of Minnesota). Slavery had been outlawed in both places. Now back in Missouri, where slavery was allowed, Scott claimed that the time he had spent in those other places had made him free.

Chief Justice Roger Taney, frail and more than 80 years old, handed down a decision that stunned many Americans. A slave was not a citizen and had no right to sue, Taney said. The Constitution, he noted, called slaves "property," property that could be taken anywhere. Taney went on to say that Congress had no right to ban slavery in any territory owned by the United States.

Throughout the North, outraged men and women labeled the ruling atrocious, and the Supreme Court criminal. "If the people obey this decision," proclaimed one newspaper editorial, "they disobey God."

When President Abraham Lincoln took office in March 1861, he promised to interpret the Constitution for "the whole people," black and white. Within weeks, however, the states of the North and South were fighting the Civil War. That four-year conflict ended slavery in the United States.

Following the Civil War, Congress passed a law providing for one annual Supreme Court term, to start on the first Monday in October, as it does today. The nation's lawmakers also ended the practice of circuit riding. The social changes resulting from the Civil War led to constitutional gains for African-Americans. For example, the Fourteenth Amendment to the Constitution, passed in 1868, guaranteed citizenship to the black population.

But it failed to bring them equality. Southern states passed laws known as black codes, which prevented blacks from owning land or moving freely in society. In 1890, Louisiana enacted a law requiring blacks and whites to ride in different railroad cars. The goal, as written in the law, was to "provide equal but separate accommodations for the white and colored races." The unwritten goal was a racist one, to keep blacks away from whites.

In 1892, a black man named Homer Plessy defied the Louisiana law. He boarded a train in

New Orleans and entered a "whites only" car, refusing to move. Plessy claimed the law was unconstitutional, and he took his case to the Supreme Court.

In handing down their decision in 1896, the justices reflected the opinion of many white Americans at that time. The Louisiana law showed "reasonableness," they said. Such laws were in keeping with the Constitution, so long as states provided railroad cars and other services that were "separate but equal."

One justice dissented, or disagreed with the Court's opinion. "Our Constitution is color-blind," said Justice John M. Harlan. "In respect of civil rights, all citizens are equal before the law." A Kentucky native, Harlan came from a family that had once owned slaves. Yet, if he held any prejudices, he refused to let them affect his understanding of the law. "The thin disguise of 'equal' accommodations for passengers in railroad coaches will not mislead anyone, nor atone for the wrong this day done," Harlan stated.

A lone dissenter, though, was powerless to change the law. African-Americans would wait more than half a century to have their rights protected by the Supreme Court.

CHAPTER 3

KEEPERS OF THE CONSTITUTION

America entered the 20th century full of optimism. Towns and cities were growing in all 48 states. Factories were turning out automobiles and household goods. During the 1920s, many workers saw their wages rise steadily. Thousands of people tried to strike it rich by investing in the stock market. Many invested on credit, using money they had not yet earned.

The good times ended abruptly in October 1929, when the stock market collapsed. The era known as the Great Depression began. This was a time of economic hardship, when countless Americans lost their jobs, their savings, and their homes. Fear and worry were everywhere.

Americans pinned their hopes on Franklin

Roosevelt, and elected him president in 1932. Roosevelt had promised the nation a "New Deal," a set of laws to revive the economy. The New Deal would create jobs and raise the prices of farmers' crops. It would regulate banks and the stock market, to protect against future depressions.

Roosevelt's popular plan made its way through Congress and became law. Then, in 1935 and 1936, the Supreme Court declared 12 New Deal laws unconstitutional. The Depression was a national crisis, but it was no reason for the justices to change their understanding of the Constitution. As Chief Justice Charles Evans Hughes explained, "Extraordinary conditions do not create or enlarge constitutional power."

An angry Roosevelt feared that the "nine old men" on the Supreme Court would never change their minds. Roosevelt came up with a scheme called "court packing." For every justice age 70 or older who refused to retire, the president wanted to add a new one. This would raise the number of justices to 15. Roosevelt claimed that the current justices had too much work to do. But, in truth, he desired to add members to the Court who favored the New Deal.

The American people reacted strongly to Roosevelt's plan. Even supporters of the New Deal wrote letters to Congress and the newspapers. The president was going too far, they said, in tampering with the Supreme Court. Congress agreed, and the number of justices remained at nine.

In time, America had a Supreme Court that favored the New Deal. Some justices came to accept Roosevelt's ideas. Others retired or died. During his more than 12 years as president, Roosevelt appointed one chief justice and eight associate justices. All supported his goals.

The New Deal brought jobs and money to thousands of unemployed people. Roosevelt was a powerful president who gave the government a lasting role in steering the economy. Still, he could not tamper with the Supreme Court.

By the time the justices were debating the New Deal legislation, they were in a home of their own. In 1932, Congress employed the architect Cass Gilbert to design a building to house the Court. Gilbert planned a structure "of dignity and importance," he said. The building would have a white marble plaza and tall columns resembling those in a Greek temple. The new Supreme Court building would remind people that the concept of democracy originated in ancient Greece.

On October 13, 1932, Chief Justice Charles Evans Hughes joined President Herbert Hoover to lay the cornerstone for the new structure. "The Republic endures and this is the symbol of its faith," said Hughes on that occasion.

The Supreme Court building was completed in 1935. For the justices, the grander, roomier quarters took some getting used to. One justice

The present Supreme Court building under construction

claimed that he and the others, in their black robes, would feel like "nine black beetles in the Temple of Karnak." He was referring to the great Egyptian building. Each justice was assigned a group of offices, called chambers, on the first floor of the new building. But for a few years, some of them preferred to do their paperwork at home.

As the century progressed, the justices continued to find themselves at the storm center of American life. The civil rights movement, with its marches and sit-ins, made important gains during the 1950s and 1960s. Several Supreme Court decisions, including the 1954 ruling on segregated schools, helped to secure the rights of African-Americans.

In 1956, the Supreme Court outlawed segregation on city buses. The case that led to that outcome began on a winter afternoon in 1955. A black seamstress named Rosa Parks, tired after a long workday, refused to give up her seat on a Montgomery, Alabama, bus so that a white man could sit down. Parks knew she would be arrested for defying the law. However, she explained, "I felt it was just something I had to do."

Parks's arrest angered Montgomery's black citizens. Led by a local minister, Martin Luther King, Jr., they boycotted the city's buses. For 381 days, they walked to work or rode in car pools rather than use a bus system that treated them unfairly. Four black residents sued the city, claiming they had been denied the treatment that white passengers received. The case reached the Supreme Court.

Just when the boycotters were about to give up, the Court settled the issue. The justices let stand a lower court decision that segregation on the city's buses was unconstitutional. The news was "a joyous daybreak to end the long night of enforced segregation in public transportation," said Martin Luther King. Four years later, the Supreme Court stated that segregation on vehicles traveling from one state to another was unconstitutional as well.

The historic civil rights cases paved the way for change, but that change often involved a further struggle. Many black students, for example, endured threats and insults to attend integrated schools. Some of the first blacks and whites to ride together on interstate bus routes were victims of violence. And in spite of the gains that have been made, racism remains a problem in American society.

The issue of school prayer also created controversy in the early 1960s. At that time, a third of the nation's school districts required children to recite a daily classroom prayer. The schoolchildren in New Hyde Park, New York, repeated a simple prayer every day, and this caused some parents to be concerned. "If the state could tell our children what to pray and when to pray and how to pray," said one father, "there was no stopping." The parents claimed it was their right to teach religion at home.

A group of parents took New York State and their school board to court. The Supreme Court ruled on the case in 1962, stating that the school prayer violated the First Amendment of the Constitution. The First Amendment gives Americans several kinds of freedom, including

The issue of school prayer became an important one in the 1960s.

the freedom to worship as they choose. The Supreme Court decision meant that school prayer was illegal not just in New York but throughout the United States.

The outcome of this case pleased many people and shocked many others. Some men and women feared it would lead to the end of religion in America. Public opinion is divided even to this day, and some religious groups are working for a new Supreme Court ruling that would return prayer to the schools.

The Supreme Court justices handed down one of their most controversial decisions in 1973, in the case of *Roe v. Wade*. A woman known to the public as Jane Roe had sued the officials of Dallas County, Texas, where she lived. Pregnant and single, Roe wished to obtain an abortion, a medical procedure to end her pregnancy. Texas law had made abortion a crime, except when it was needed to save a woman's life.

The woman hoped the Supreme Court would declare Texas's law unconstitutional. She and her lawyers believed that the Fourteenth Amendment, which extended citizenship and liberty to all Americans, protected a woman's right to choose abortion.

The Court agreed, declaring that states could no longer ban abortion. But although the justices announced that decision two decades ago, abortion remains a topic of heated debate. Many people insist that a woman must have control

The anonymous "Jane Roe" of Roe v. Wade *returned to the Supreme Court in the late 1980s as a spectator.*

over her body. Many others believe that ending a pregnancy amounts to murder. They hope the Court will one day reverse its decision in *Roe v. Wade*.

The Supreme Court again made news in 1974. In that year, the Court forced a president of the United States to obey the law. The scandal known as Watergate began in June 1972, when President Richard Nixon, a Republican, was running for re-election. Seven members of the president's re-election committee were arrested. They had broken into offices of the Democratic Party at the Watergate Hotel in Washington, D.C.

In the months ahead, the nation learned that some of Nixon's top aides had known about the break-in before it happened. Many Americans wondered, had the president known? Nixon claimed he had not. But then people asked, was he telling the truth?

Tapes of conversations held in the president's office had the answers, and a U.S. district court ordered Nixon to turn over those tapes. The president refused, claiming that the Constitution gave him the right to do so. He said he was "answerable to the nation, but not to the courts."

The Supreme Court heard arguments in the

case of *United States v. Nixon* in July 1974. Leon Jaworski, the attorney speaking for the United States, stressed the justices' role as keepers of the Constitution. If the president is free to use the Constitution any way he likes, Jaworski asked, "what then becomes of our constitutional form of government?"

Two weeks later, Chief Justice Warren Burger read the Court's decision. The president must surrender his tapes, Burger said. Those tapes made it clear Nixon had known about the break-in for months before it took place. On August 9, Richard Nixon resigned as president. Although he had broken the law, he was never arrested or brought to trial. The new president, Gerald Ford, pardoned Nixon for any crimes he had committed. Ford wanted Americans to put Watergate behind them and look toward the future.

CHAPTER 4

THE JUSTICES AT WORK

The Supreme Court justices appear before the public as judges in flowing black robes, but their jobs require them to wear many hats. They are first and foremost judges, but they are scholars, writers, and editors as well. They need to be good listeners, persuasive speakers, and people who like to read. And they must be tireless workers.

The justices hear about 170 cases each year. These cases reach the high court in three ways. First, the Supreme Court has original jurisdiction, or acts as a trial court, in a small number of cases. These cases arise when one state brings legal action against another, or when a state and the federal government are involved in a legal dispute.

The second group of cases consists of mandatory appeals, which the Supreme Court must hear. For example, the Court is required to review a case if a federal court has declared a state law unconstitutional.

Most cases, however, reach the Supreme Court in the third way, through a method called certiorari. The legal term *certiorari* comes from a Latin phrase, *certiorari volumus,* meaning, "we wish to be informed." People who want the Supreme Court to review their case must submit a written request, known as a writ of certiorari. Between 4,000 and 5,000 writs of certiorari reach the Supreme Court every year.

Each justice employs a staff of law clerks, young attorneys just starting their careers. The law clerks help the justices by reading through the "writs of cert." They then write a summary of each case. After reading one of these summaries, a justice may think that the decision of a lower court was incorrect. Or it may seem that a

The justices' conference room, which is closed to the public. A portrait of John Marshall hangs over the fireplace.

case has constitutional importance. The justice then places the case on a list for discussion.

The justices discuss the list during conferences held each Wednesday afternoon and all day Friday. These meetings are highly secret. No one is allowed inside the conference room except the

justices themselves. They shake hands at the door, as they have since the 1880s. Then they take their seats at a long table beside a fireplace. A portrait of John Marshall appears to look down on them from an oak-paneled wall. Carts piled high with legal books and papers fill the room so the justices will have all the information they need as the meeting proceeds.

As presiding officer of the Court, the chief justice presents a summary of each case on the discussion list. He states whether he thinks the Court should hear the case, and why. The other justices present their opinions, and a vote is taken. The justices elect to hear cases according to the "rule of four." If four or more justices vote to review a case, it will come before the Supreme Court.

Because their actions affect the lives of many people, the justices cast their votes with much thought, care, and humility. Chief Justice Rehnquist admits thinking, when first faced with this responsibility, "Who am I to be doing this?"

Once the Court votes to hear a case, the lawyers for each side prepare briefs for the justices to read. A brief is a written explanation of the legal questions in the case, along with the lawyer's opinion on how the case should be decided. Other interested persons may submit briefs as well. The justices will read the briefs carefully before hearing the lawyers argue the case in Court.

The Supreme Court holds seven two-week sittings per term, separated by recesses of about two weeks. The public may call the Court to learn when cases are scheduled to be heard. The justices' conferences may be private, but the Court in session is a public event. The lawyer on each side has one half hour to speak. In very important cases, however, the lawyers are given more time. The attorneys arguing the case *United States v. Nixon,* for instance, spoke for three hours each.

The oral arguments give the justices a clearer understanding of the case. "Often my whole notion of what a case is about crystallizes at oral argument," said Justice William J. Brennan, Jr., before he retired in 1990. "This happens even though I read the briefs before." The justices pose difficult questions, and they expect quick, informative answers. "We are learning, but we are trying to decide it, too," said Justice Byron White, who spent 31 years on the Supreme Court.

After the briefs have been read and the oral arguments heard, the justices talk about the case in their private conference. Some justices express their thoughts calmly and in a few words, while others speak at length. Justice Felix Frankfurter, a member of the Court from 1939 until 1962, was a law professor before he became a justice. He seemed to miss the classroom, for he often gave dramatic lectures to his colleagues. "Felix, I came here this morning absolutely certain I would vote in favor of your position," Justice William O. Douglas once told him. "Now you've talked me out of it."

Once they have aired their views, the justices cast their votes and decide who will write the Court's opinion. A justice may write a dissenting opinion, as Justice Harlan did in the case of Homer Plessy. Such opinions have no effect on the present case, but they may have future importance. Dissent, said former Chief Justice Hughes, appeals "to the intelligence of a future day," when the Court may correct the error that the dissenting justice thinks has been made.

A Supreme Court justice writes between 13 and 18 opinions a year. Writing opinions is a lengthy process that takes place in the weeks between sessions. Once a justice is pleased with his or her work on an opinion, the draft is passed along to the other justices who voted in the same way. They act as tough editors, reading the draft and asking the writer to make changes. Then they read it and comment again. A written opinion often goes through seven or eight drafts before the justices are satisfied that it is ready to be announced in Court. Occasionally, the number of drafts can be as high as 20.

The term of the Court, which begins on the first Monday in October, ends in April. But the justices spend several more weeks writing opinions for the cases they heard during the year. Then they enjoy a short vacation before returning to work in July. Through steaming summer days, they are hard at work in their chambers. They read through the many writs of certiorari that have recently arrived, preparing for the new term in October. Interpreting the Constitution is a complex, never-ending task.

CHAPTER 5

THIS HONORABLE COURT

People arrive early on days when the Supreme
Court is sitting. They hurry past the Library of
Congress, library to the nation, and the U.S.
Capitol, the sprawling, domed structure in which
laws are made. They head toward the gleaming
whiteness of the Supreme Court building, which
takes up a full square city block. Soon, a crowd
has gathered, waiting to see the Supreme Court
in action. The people line up to view a spectacle
that Chief Justice Rehnquist calls "one of the
best tourist sights in Washington."

Even before the visitors move inside, they
see much that impresses—a sleek marble plaza,
two rows of columns holding up the heavy roof,
and broad, stately stairs. High above their heads,

the building's ornate facade bears a simple motto that expresses the Supreme Court's goal: "Equal Justice Under Law." It is a goal Thurgood Marshall echoed when he became a justice of the Court.

The visitors mount the stairs, passing two statues that seem to guard the entrance to the Supreme Court. The seated stone figures represent the Contemplation of Justice and the Guardian, or Authority of Law. Every year, 500,000 men, women, and children pass through the heavy bronze doors of the Supreme Court. The eight panels in these doors depict scenes from the history of law, from ancient Greece and Rome through the founding of the United States.

Once inside, people often feel swallowed up by white marble. They are in the Court's main corridor, or Great Hall, where marble covers the ceiling, walls, and floor. Marble columns line the walls, along with busts of the 15 former chief justices. Visitors gaze at the likenesses of John

A view of the great exterior columns

The side entrance doors to the Courtroom

Jay, the first chief justice; Roger Taney, who presided over the Court during the Dred Scott case; and Earl Warren, the justice who read the Court's opinion in *Brown v. Board of Education*.

People walk from the past into the present as

The actual Courtroom

they step into the Courtroom, where the current justices work on behalf of the nation. It is a large room, 82 feet by 91 feet, with a ceiling 44 feet high. The carpet of red, gold, and black repeats the rosette pattern that has been carved into the ceiling. As the spectators take their seats, they face the raised bench where the justices will sit, positioned before four marble columns and red velvet drapes.

The bench remains vacant until precisely 10:00 A.M., when the crier of the Court bangs once with a gavel to call the room to attention. "The Honorable, the Chief Justice and the Associate Justices of the Supreme Court of the United States!" announces the crier. A ripple of excitement passes through the room as the justices step from behind the velvet curtains and promptly take their seats.

Chief Justice Rehnquist sits at the center of the bench. The associate justice with the most years of service occupies the chair at Rehnquist's left. The other justices have seats assigned according to their time on the Court. Before Thurgood Marshall was appointed to the Supreme Court, every justice had been a white man. Clarence Thomas, also an African-American, joined the Court following Thurgood Marshall's retirement. Two female justices now sit behind the bench as well. President Ronald Reagan named Sandra Day O'Connor to the

The first woman appointed to the Supreme Court, Justice Sandra Day O'Connor

Court in 1981, and President Bill Clinton appointed Ruth Bader Ginsburg in 1993.

Using an old word meaning "hear ye," the crier speaks again. "Oyez, oyez, oyez. All persons having business before the Supreme Court of the

United States are admonished to draw near and give their attention, for the Court is now sitting. God save the United States and this Honorable Court!"

The crier pounds with the gavel once more, and the business of the Supreme Court begins. For two hours, the justices listen to lawyers' oral arguments and question the attorneys on points of law. After an hour's break, they hear more oral arguments in the afternoon.

Not everyone who comes to the Supreme Court wants to sit through two hours of legal arguments. Many visitors take a spot in the "three-minute line." They will have a chance to view the proceedings for a brief three minutes before marshals of the Court usher them out of the Courtroom.

The Supreme Court welcomes visitors whether or not the justices are seated at their bench. On days when the Court is not sitting, staff members give lectures in the Courtroom.

Ruth Bader Ginsburg holds a copy of the Constitution during her successful Senate confirmation hearings.

During these short talks, the staff members explain the Court's workings and history. They point out features of the Courtroom, such as the sculpted bands on the north and south walls that depict great lawgivers from history. A marble panel over the Courtroom's main entrance contains a figure representing Justice, flanked by the figures of Wisdom and Truth. This panel also shows the powers of evil—qualities like corruption and deceit—being offset by the powers of good—security, charity, and peace.

Many adults and children seek out the exhibits on the ground floor of the Supreme Court building, where portraits of justices line the walls. In the center of the exhibit area stands a massive bronze statue of John Marshall, the "great chief justice." This statue first stood in the U.S. Capitol, where it was placed in 1884. In 1982, it found a new home at the Supreme Court.

Visitors also see changing exhibits on the history of the United States and the Supreme Court. They might see a reproduction of an early draft of the Declaration of Independence in Thomas Jefferson's own handwriting, postage stamps honoring past justices, or a sculpture of the justices seated at their bench. Young people enjoy the dizzying sight of a five-story spiral staircase. The Supreme Court has two of these marble sets of stairs. They are designed to be self-supporting—each step helps to hold those above and below it in place. Only a few staircases like this are known to exist in the world.

At one end of the exhibit area, a film plays again and again. In words and pictures, the film tells the story of the Supreme Court from its beginnings in the 1700s through the present.

For many Americans, a trip to Washington, D.C., would not be complete without a stop at the Supreme Court. Justice Lewis F. Powell, Jr., who served on the Court from 1972 until 1987, summed up the feelings of his fellow citizens

A view looking down the building's famous spiral staircase

toward their highest court. "The American people have respected the courts," he said, "and they have placed special trust and confidence in the Supreme Court." The Supreme Court has earned that trust and confidence. For more than 200 years, it has worked to secure personal liberty and shape the government of the United States.

THE SUPREME COURT: A HISTORICAL TIME LINE

1787   Delegates from 12 of the 13 states draft the Constitution, which calls for a Supreme Court.

1788   The states ratify the Constitution.

1789   President George Washington signs the First Judiciary Act. Washington appoints the first Supreme Court Justices; the Senate confirms his choices.

1790   The Supreme Court meets for the first time, in New York City.

1791   Philadelphia becomes the capital, and the Supreme Court meets there.

1795   John Jay resigns as the first chief justice.

1801   The federal government moves to Washington, D.C. The Supreme Court meets in the U.S. Capitol. John Marshall is appointed chief justice.

1803   The Supreme Court rules in the case *Marbury v. Madison,* establishing its right to decide the constitutionality of laws.

1835   John Marshall dies.

1854   In deciding the Dred Scott case, the Supreme Court rules that slaves are not citizens.

1861-1865   The Civil War years. One result of the war is the end of slavery in the United States.

1868   The Fourteenth Amendment extends citizenship to all Americans.

1896   The Supreme Court hands down its opinion in

the case of Homer Plessy; the Court allows "separate but equal" services for the black and white races.

1929 The Great Depression begins.

1932 Congress hires architect Cass Gilbert to design a new Supreme Court building. Chief Justice Charles Evans Hughes and President Herbert Hoover lay the cornerstone. Franklin Roosevelt is elected president, promising a "New Deal" for Americans.

1935 The Supreme Court declares the first New Deal laws to be unconstitutional. The Supreme Court building is completed.

1936 The nation rejects Roosevelt's court-packing plan.

1954 The Supreme Court decides the case of *Brown v. Board of Education*. In ending school segregation, the Court reverses its 1896 "separate but equal" ruling.

1956 The Court outlaws segregation on city buses.

1960 Segregation on interstate transportation is now unconstitutional.

1962 The justices rule that school prayer is in conflict with the Constitution.

1967 Thurgood Marshall becomes the nation's first African-American Supreme Court justice.

1973 The Supreme Court declares that states may not ban abortion.

1974 The Court requires President Richard Nixon to surrender tapes of conversations in his White House office. The tapes prove Nixon had knowledge of the Watergate break-in. Nixon resigns.

1981 President Ronald Reagan appoints Sandra Day O'Connor to be the first female Supreme Court justice.

1991 Thurgood Marshall resigns from the Supreme Court due to age and ill health. Clarence Thomas joins the Court.

1993 Thurgood Marshall dies. The second female Supreme Court justice, Ruth Bader Ginsberg, is appointed by President Bill Clinton.

THE SUPREME COURT JUSTICES

The Chief Justices

Name	Years of Service	Name	Years of Service
John Jay	1789-1795	Edward D. White	1910-1921
John Rutledge*	1795	William H. Taft	1921-1930
Oliver Ellsworth	1796-1809	Charles E. Hughes	1930-1941
John Marshall	1801-1835	Harlan F. Stone	1941-1946
Roger B. Taney	1836-1864	Fred M. Vinson	1946-1953
Salmon P. Chase	1864-1873	Earl Warren	1953-1969
Morrison R. Waite	1874-1888	Warren E. Burger	1969-1986
Melville W. Fuller	1888-1910	William H. Rehnquist	1986-present

*Although Rutledge served briefly as chief justice, the Senate rejected his appointment.

The Associate Justices

Name	Years of Service	Name	Years of Service
James Wilson	1789-1798	John McLean	1830-1861
John Rutledge	1790-1791	Henry Baldwin	1830-1844
William Cushing	1790-1810	James M. Wayne	1835-1867
John Blair	1790-1796	Philip P. Barbour	1836-1841
James Iredell	1790-1799	John Catron	1837-1865
Thomas Johnson	1792-1793	John McKinley	1838-1852
William Paterson	1793-1806	Peter V. Daniel	1842-1860
Samuel Chase	1796-1811	Samuel Nelson	1845-1872
Bushrod Washington	1799-1829	Levi Woodbury	1845-1851
Alfred Moore	1800-1804	Robert C. Grier	1846-1870
William Johnson	1804-1834	Benjamin R. Curtis	1851-1857
Henry B. Livingston	1806-1823	John A. Campbell	1853-1861
Thomas Todd	1807-1826	Nathan Clifford	1858-1881
Gabriel Duvall	1811-1835	Noah H. Swayne	1862-1881
Joseph Story	1811-1845	Samuel F. Miller	1862-1890
Smith Thompson	1823-1843	David Davis	1862-1877
Robert Trimble	1826-1828	Stephen J. Field	1863-1897

William Strong	1870-1880	Benjamin N. Cardozo	1932-1938
Joseph P. Bradley	1870-1892	Hugo L. Black	1937-1971
Ward Hunt	1873-1882	Stanley F. Reed	1938-1957
John M. Harlan	1877-1911	Felix Frankfurter	1939-1962
William B. Woods	1881-1887	William O. Douglas	1939-1975
Stanley Matthews	1881-1889	Frank Murphy	1940-1949
Horace Gray	1882-1902	James F. Byrnes	1941-1942
Samuel Blatchford	1882-1893	Robert H. Jackson	1941-1954
Lucius Q. C. Lamar	1888-1893	Wiley B. Rutledge	1943-1949
David J. Brewer	1890-1910	Harold H. Burton	1945-1958
Henry B. Brown	1891-1906	Tom C. Clark	1949-1967
George Shiras, Jr.	1892-1903	Sherman Minton	1949-1956
Howell E. Jackson	1893-1895	John M. Harlan	1955-1971
Edward D. White	1894-1910	William J. Brennan, Jr.	1956-1990
Rufus W. Peckham	1896-1909	Charles E. Whittaker	1957-1962
Joseph McKenna	1898-1925	Potter Stewart	1958-1981
Oliver W. Holmes, Jr.	1902-1932	Byron R. White	1962-1993
William R. Day	1903-1922	Arthur J. Goldberg	1962-1965
William H. Moody	1906-1910	Abe Fortas	1965-1969
Horace H. Lurton	1910-1914	Thurgood Marshall	1967-1991
Charles E. Hughes	1910-1916	Harry A. Blackmun	1970-1994
Willis Van Devanter	1911-1937	Lewis F. Powell, Jr.	1972-1987
Joseph R. Lamar	1911-1916	William H. Rehnquist	1972-1986
Mahlon Pitney	1912-1922	John P. Stevens	1975-present
James C. McReynolds	1914-1941	Sandra Day O'Connor	1981-present
Louis D. Brandeis	1916-1939	Antonin Scalia	1986-present
John H. Clarke	1916-1922	Anthony Kennedy	1988-present
George Sutherland	1922-1938	David Souter	1990-present
Pierce Butler	1923-1939	Clarence Thomas	1991-present
Edward T. Sanford	1923-1930	Ruth Bader Ginsburg	1993-present
Harlan F. Stone	1925-1941	Stephen G. Breyer	1994-present
Owen J. Roberts	1930-1945		

(Note: John Rutledge, Edward D. White, Charles Evans Hughes, Harlan F. Stone, and William H. Rehnquist held the position of associate justice before serving as

VISITOR INFORMATION

Hours
> 9:00 A.M. to 4:30 P.M., weekdays
> Closed holidays

Observing the Supreme Court in Session
> On days when the Court is in session, visitors may view the proceedings between 10:00 A.M. and noon, or between 1:00 P.M. and 3:00 P.M. Because space is limited, visitors should plan to arrive one hour early. It is also possible to make a brief, three-minute visit to the Courtroom.

Visiting the Courtroom at Other Times
> Between 9:30 A.M. and 3:30 P.M., Supreme Court staff members present a 15-minute lecture inside the Courtroom.

The Exhibit Area
> The ground-floor exhibit area contains a statue of Chief Justice John Marshall, portraits of former justices, and displays on the Supreme Court's past. A continuously running film explains the Court's history and operations.

For more information, contact:
> The Supreme Court
> 1 First Street NE
> Washington, DC 20543
> (202) 479-3000

INDEX